Rules of Procedure of the Antarctic Treaty Consultative Meeting and the Committee for Environmental Protection

Updated: June 2016

ISSN 2362-2156

Secretariat of the Antarctic Treaty
Secrétariat du Traité sur L'Antarctique
Секретариат Договора об Антарктике
Secretaría del Tratado Antártico

Rules of Procedure of the Antarctic Treaty Consultative Meeting and the Committee for Environmental Protection

Updated: June 2016

Secretariat of the Antarctic Treaty

Buenos Aires

2016

Rules of Procedure of the Antarctic Treaty Consultative Meeting and the Committee for Environmental Protection. Updated: June 2016.

Buenos Aires : Secretariat of the Antarctic Treaty, 2016.

41 p.

1. International law. 2. Antarctic Treaty System. 3. International agreements.

ISBN 978-987-4024-14-5

ISSN 2362-2156

DDC 341.2/9

Published by:

Secretariat of the Antarctic Treaty
Secrétariat du Traité sur L'Antarctique
Секретариат Договора об Антарктике
Secretaría del Tratado Antártico

Maipú 757, piso 4

C1006ACI - Ciudad Autónoma

Buenos Aires - Argentina

Tel: +54 11 4320-4250

Fax: +54 11 4320-4253

This book is also available from *www.ats.aq* (digital version) and online retailers.

ISSN 2362-2156

CONTENTS

Revised Rules of Procedure for the Antarctic Treaty Consultative Meeting (2016)

1.   Meetings held pursuant to Article IX of the Antarctic Treaty shall be known as Antarctic Treaty Consultative Meetings. Contracting Parties entitled to participate in those Meetings shall be referred to as "Consultative Parties"; other Contracting Parties which may have been invited to attend those Meetings shall be referred to as "non-Consultative Parties". The Executive Secretary of the Secretariat of the Antarctic Treaty shall be referred to as the "Executive Secretary".

2.   The Representatives of the Commission for the Conservation of Antarctic Marine Living Resources, the Scientific Committee on Antarctic Research and the Council of Managers of National Antarctic Programs, invited to attend those Meetings in accordance with Rule 31, shall be referred to as "Observers".

Representation

3.   Each Consultative Party shall be represented by a delegation composed of a Representative and such Alternate Representatives, Advisers and other persons as each State may deem necessary. Each non-Consultative Party which has been invited to attend a Consultative Meeting shall be represented by a delegation composed of a Representative and such other persons as it may deem necessary within such numerical limit as may from time to time be determined by the Host Government in consultation with the Consultative Parties. The Commission for the Conservation of Antarctic Marine Living Resources, the Scientific Committee on Antarctic Research and the Council of Managers of National Antarctic Programs shall be represented by their respective Chairman or President, or other persons appointed to this end. The names of members of delegations and of the observers shall be communicated to the Host Government prior to the opening of the Meeting.

4.   The order of precedence of the delegations shall be in accordance with the alphabet in the language of the Host Government, all delegations of non-Consultative Parties following after those of Consultative Parties, and all delegations of observers following after non-Consultative Parties.

Officers

5.   A Representative of the Host Government shall be the Temporary Chairman of the Meeting and shall preside until the Meeting elects a Chairman.

6.   At its inaugural session, a Chairman from one of the Consultative Parties shall be elected. The other Representatives of Consultative Parties shall serve as Vice-Chairmen of the Meeting in order of precedence. The Chairman normally shall preside at all plenary sessions. If he is absent from any session or part thereof, the Vice-Chairmen, rotating on the basis of the order of precedence as established by Rule 4, shall preside during each such session.

Secretariat

7.   The Executive Secretary shall act as Secretary to the Meeting. He or she shall be responsible, with the assistance of the Host Government, for providing secretariat services for the meeting, as provided in Article 2 of Measure 1 (2003), as provisionally applied by Decision 2 (2003) until Measure 1 becomes effective.

Sessions

8.   The opening plenary session shall be held in public, other sessions shall be held in private, unless the Meeting shall determine otherwise.

Committees and Working Groups

9.   The Meeting, to facilitate its work, may establish such committees as it may deem necessary for the performance of its functions, defining their terms of reference.

10.   The committees shall operate under the Rules of Procedure of the Meeting, except where they are inapplicable.

11.   Working Groups may be established by the Meeting, or its committees to deal with various agenda items. The Meeting will determine the provisional arrangements for Working Groups at the end of each Consultative Meeting, when it approves the preliminary agenda for the subsequent Meeting (under Rule 36). These arrangements will include

      a)   the establishment of Working Group(s) for the subsequent Meeting;

b)   the appointment of Working Group Chair(s); and

c)   the allocation of agenda items to each Working Group.

Where the Meeting decides that a Working Group should be continued for more than one year, the Chair(s) of those Working Group(s) may be appointed for a period of one or two consecutive Meetings in the first instance. Working Group Chairs may subsequently be appointed for further terms of one or two years, but will not serve for more than four consecutive years in the same Working Group.

Should the Meeting be unable to appoint a Working Group Chair(s) for the subsequent Meeting, a Chair(s) shall be appointed at the beginning of the subsequent Meeting.

Conduct of Business

12.   A quorum shall be constituted by two-thirds of the Representatives of Consultative Parties participating in the Meeting.

13.   The Chairman shall exercise the powers of his office in accordance with customary practice. He shall see to the observance of the Rules of Procedure and the maintenance of proper order. The Chairman, in the exercise of his functions, remains under the authority of the Meeting.

14.   Subject to Rule 28, no Representative may address the Meeting without having previously obtained the permission of the Chairman and the Chairman shall call upon speakers in the order in which they signify their desire to speak. The Chairman may call a speaker to order if his remarks are not relevant to the subject under discussion.

15.   During the discussion of any matter, a Representative of a Consultative Party may rise to a point of order and the point of order shall be decided immediately by the Chairman in accordance with the Rules of Procedure. A Representative of a Consultative Party may appeal against the ruling of the Chairman. The appeal shall be put to a vote immediately, and the Chairman's ruling shall stand unless over-ruled by a majority of the Representatives of Consultative Parties present and voting. A Representative of a Consultative party rising to a point of order shall not speak on the substance of the matter under discussion.

16.   The Meeting may limit the time to be allotted to each speaker, and the number of times he may speak on any subject. When the debate is thus limited and

a Representative has spoken his allotted time, the Chairman shall call him to order without delay.

17.   During the discussion of any matter, a Representative of a Consultative Party may move the adjournment of the debate on the item under discussion. In addition to the proposer of the motion, Representatives of two Consultative Parties may speak in favour of, and two against, the motion, after which the motion shall be put to the vote immediately. The Chairman may limit the time to be allowed to speakers under this Rule.

18.   A Representative of a Consultative Party may at any time move the closure of the debate in the item under discussion, whether or not any other Representative has signified his wish to speak. Permission to speak on the closure of the debate shall be accorded only to Representatives of two Consultative Parties opposing the closure, after which the motion shall be put to the vote immediately. If the Meeting is in favour of the closure, the Chairman shall declare the closure of the debate. The Chairman may limit the time to be allowed to speakers under this Rule. (This Rule shall not apply to debate in committees.)

19.   During the discussion of any matter, a Representative of a Consultative Party may move the suspension or adjournment of the Meeting. Such motions shall not be debated, but shall be put to the vote immediately. The Chairman may limit the time to be allowed to the speaker moving the suspension or adjournment of the Meeting.

20.   Subject to Rule 15, the following motions shall have precedence in the following order over all other proposals or motions before the Meeting:

a)   to suspend the Meeting;

b)   to adjourn the Meeting;

c)   to adjourn the debate on the item under discussion;

d)   for the closure of the debate on the item under discussion.

21.   Decisions of the Meeting on all matters of procedure shall be taken by a majority of the Representatives of Consultative Parties participating in the Meeting, each of whom shall have one vote.

Languages

22.   English, French, Russian and Spanish shall be the official languages of the Meeting.

23.   Any Representative may speak in a language other than the official languages. However, in such cases he shall provide for interpretation into one of the official languages.

Measures, Decisions, and Resolutions and Final Report

24.   Without prejudice to Rule 21, Measures, Decisions and Resolutions, as referred to in Decision 1 (1995), shall be adopted by the Representatives of all Consultative Parties present and will thereafter be subject to the provisions of Decision 1 (1995).

25.   The final report shall also contain a brief account of the proceedings of the Meeting. It will be approved by a majority of the Representatives of Consultative Parties present and shall be transmitted by the Executive Secretary to Governments of all Consultative and non-Consultative Parties which have been invited to take part in the Meeting for their consideration.

26.   Notwithstanding Rule 25, the Executive Secretary, immediately following the closure of the Consultative Meeting, shall notify all Consultative Parties of all Measures, Decisions and Resolutions taken and send them authenticated copies of the definitive texts in an appropriate language of the Meeting. In respect to a Measure adopted under the procedures of Article 6 or 8 of Annex V of the Protocol, the respective notification shall also include the time period for approval of that Measure.

Non-Consultative Parties

27.   Representatives of non-Consultative Parties, if invited to attend a Consultative Meeting, may be present at:

a)   all plenary sessions of the Meeting; and

b)   all formal Committees or Working Groups, comprising all Consultative Parties, unless a Representative of a Consultative Party requests otherwise in any particular case.

28.   The relevant Chairman may invite a Representative of a non-Consultative Party to address the Meeting, Committee or Working group which he is attending, unless a Representative of a Consultative Party requests otherwise. The Chairman shall at any time give priority to Representatives of Consultative Parties who signify

their desire to speak and may, in inviting Representatives of non-Consultative Parties to address the Meeting, limit the time to be allotted to each speaker and the number of times he may speak on any subject.

29.   Non-Consultative Parties are not entitled to participate in the taking of decisions.

30.

   a) Non-Consultative Parties may submit documents to the Secretariat for distribution to the Meeting as information documents. Such documents shall be relevant to matters under Committee consideration at the Meeting.

   b) Unless a Representative of a Consultative Party requests otherwise such documents shall be available only in the language or languages in which they were submitted.

Antarctic Treaty System Observers

31.   The observers referred to in Rule 2 shall attend the Meetings for the specific purpose of reporting on:

   a) in the case of the Commission for the Conservation of Antarctic Marine Living Resources, developments in its area of competence.

   b) in the case of the Scientific Committee on Antarctic Research:

      i)   the general proceedings of SCAR;

      ii)   matters within the competence of SCAR under the Convention for the Conservation of Antarctic Seals;

      iii) such publications and reports as may have been published or prepared in accordance with Recommendations IX-19 and VI-9 respectively.

   c) in the case of the Council of Managers of National Antarctic Programs, the activities within its area of competence.

32.   Observers may be present at:

   a) the plenary sessions of the Meeting at which the respective Report is considered;

b) formal committees or working groups, comprising all Contracting Parties at which the respective Report is considered, unless a Representative of a Consultative Party requests otherwise in any particular case.

33. Following the presentation of the pertinent Report, the relevant Chairman may invite the observer to address the Meeting at which it is being considered once again, unless a Representative of a Consultative Party requests otherwise. The Chairman may allot a time limit for such interventions.

34. Observers are not entitled to participate in the taking of decisions.

35. Observers may submit their Report and/or documents relevant to matters contained therein to the Secretariat, for distribution to the Meeting as working papers.

Agenda for Consultative Meetings

36. At the end of each Consultative Meeting, the Host Government of that Meeting shall prepare a preliminary agenda for the next Consultative Meeting. If approved by the Meeting, the preliminary agenda for the next Meeting shall be annexed to the Final Report of the Meeting.

37. Any Contracting Party may propose supplementary items for the preliminary agenda by informing the Host Government for the forthcoming Consultative Meeting no later than 180 days before the beginning of the Meeting; each proposal shall be accompanied by an explanatory memorandum. The Host Government shall draw the attention of all Contracting Parties to this Rule no later than 210 days before the Meeting.

38. The Host Government shall prepare a provisional agenda for the Consultative Meeting. The provisional agenda shall contain:

a) all items on the preliminary agenda decided in accordance with Rule 36; and

b) all items the inclusion of which has been requested by a Contracting Party pursuant to Rule 37.

Not later than 120 days before the Meeting, the Host Government shall transmit to all the Contracting Parties the provisional agenda, together with explanatory memoranda and any other papers related thereto.

Experts from International Organisations

39.   At the end of each Consultative Meeting, the Meeting shall decide which international organisations having a scientific or technical interest in Antarctica shall be invited to designate an expert to attend the forthcoming Meeting in order to assist it in its substantive work.

40.   Any Contracting Party may thereafter propose that an invitation be extended to other international organisations having a scientific or technical interest in Antarctica to assist the Meeting in its substantive work; each such proposal shall be submitted to the Host Government for that Meeting not later than 180 days before the beginning of the Meeting and shall be accompanied by a memorandum setting out the basis for the proposal.

41.   The Host Government shall transmit these proposals to all Contracting Parties in accordance with the procedure in Rule 38. Any Consultative Party which wishes to object to a proposal shall do so not less than 90 days before the Meeting.

42.   Unless such an objection has been received, the Host Government shall extend invitations to international organisations identified in accordance with Rules 39 and 40 and shall request each international organisation to communicate the name of the designated expert to the Host Government prior to the opening of the Meeting. All such experts may attend the Meeting during consideration of all items, except for those items relating to the operation of the Antarctic Treaty System which are identified by the previous Meeting or upon adoption of the agenda.

43.   The relevant Chairman, with the agreement of all the Consultative Parties, may invite an expert to address the meeting he is attending. The Chairman shall at any time give priority to Representatives of Consultative Parties or non-Consultative Parties or Observers referred to in Rule 31 who signify their desire to speak, and may in inviting an expert to address the Meeting limit the time to be allotted to him and the number of times he may speak on any subject.

44.   Experts are not entitled to participate in the taking of decisions.

45.

a) Experts may, in respect of the relevant agenda item, submit documents to the Secretariat for distribution to the Meeting as information documents.

b) Unless a Representative of a Consultative Party requests otherwise, such documents shall be available only in the language or languages in which they were submitted.

Intersessional Consultations

46.   Intersessionally, the Executive Secretary shall, within his/her competence as established under Measure 1 (2003) and associated instruments that govern the operation of the Secretariat, consult the Consultative Parties, when legally required to do so under relevant instruments of the ATCM and when the exigencies of the circumstances require action to be taken before the opening of the next ATCM, using the following procedure:

a) Each Consultative Party shall keep the Executive Secretary advised on an ongoing basis of its Representative and any Alternate Representatives, who shall have authority to speak for their Consultative Party for the purposes of intersessional consultations.

b) The Executive Secretary shall maintain a list of the Representatives and Alternate Representatives and ensure that it remains current.

c) When intersessional consultations are required, the Executive Secretary shall transmit the relevant information and any proposed action to all Consultative Parties through their Representatives and any Alternate Representatives designated under paragraph (a) above, indicating an appropriate date by which responses are requested.

d) The Executive Secretary shall ensure that all Consultative Parties acknowledge the receipt of such transmission.

e) Each Consultative Party shall consider the matter and communicate its reply, if any, to the Executive Secretary through its Representative or an Alternate Representative by the specified date.

f) The Executive Secretary after informing the Consultative Parties of the result of the consultations, may proceed to take the proposed action if no Consultative Party has objected.

g) The Executive Secretary shall keep a record of the intersessional consultations, including results of those intersessional consultations and the actions taken by him/her and shall reflect these results and actions in his/her report to the ATCM for its review.

47.   Intersessionally, when a request for information about the activities of the ATCM is received from an international organisation having a scientific or technical interest in Antarctica, the Executive Secretary shall coordinate a response, using the following procedure:

a) The Executive Secretary shall transmit the request and a first draft response to all Consultative Parties through their Representatives and any Alternate Representatives designated under Rule 46 (a), proposing to answer the request, and including an appropriate date by which Consultative Parties should either (1) indicate that it would not be appropriate to answer, or (2) provide comments to the first draft response. The date shall give a reasonable amount of time to provide comments, taking into account any deadlines set by the initial requests for information. If a Consultative Party indicates that a response would not be appropriate, the Executive Secretary shall send only a formal response, acknowledging the request without going into the substance of the matter.

b) If there is no objection to proceeding and if comments are provided before the date specified in the transmission referred to in paragraph (a) above, the Executive Secretary shall revise the response in light of the comments and transmit the revised response to all Consultative Parties, including an appropriate date by which reactions are requested.

c) If any further comments are provided before the date specified in the transmission referred to in paragraph (b) above, the Executive Secretary shall repeat the procedure referred to in paragraph (b) above until no further comments are provided.

d) If no comments are provided before the date specified in a transmission referred to in paragraph (a), (b) or (c) above, the Executive Secretary shall circulate a final version and shall request both an active digital "read"-confirmation and an active digital "accept"-confirmation from each Consultative Party, suggesting a date by which the "accept"-confirmation should be received. The Executive Secretary shall keep the Consultative Parties informed about the progress of received confirmations. After receipt of "accept"-confirmations from all Consultative Parties the Executive Secretary shall sign and send the response to the international organisation concerned, on behalf of all Consultative Parties, and shall provide a copy of the signed response to all Consultative Parties.

e) Any Consultative Party may, at any stage of this process, ask for more time for consideration.

f) Any Consultative Party may, at any stage of this process, indicate that it would not be appropriate to respond to the request. In this case the Executive Secretary shall send only a formal response, acknowledging the request without going into the substance of the matter.

Meeting Documents

48. Working Papers shall refer to papers submitted by Consultative Parties that require discussion and action at a Meeting and papers submitted by Observers referred to in Rule 2.

49. Secretariat Papers shall refer to papers prepared by the Secretariat pursuant to a mandate established at a Meeting, or which would, in the view of the Executive Secretary, help inform the Meeting or assist in its operation.

50. Information Papers shall refer to:

- Papers submitted by Consultative Parties or Observers that provide information in support of a Working Paper or that are relevant to discussions at a Meeting;

- Papers submitted by Non-Consultative Parties that are relevant to discussions at a Meeting; and

- Papers submitted by Experts that are relevant to discussions at a Meeting.

51. Background Papers shall refer to papers submitted by any participant that will not be introduced in a Meeting, but that are submitted for the purpose of formally providing information.

52. Procedures for the submission, translation and distribution of documents are annexed to these Rules of Procedure.

Amendments

53. These Rules of Procedure may be amended by a two-thirds majority of the Representatives of Consultative Parties participating in the Meeting. This Rule shall not apply to Rules 24, 27, 29, 34, 39-42, 44, and 46, amendments of which shall

Rules of Procedure of the ATCM and the CEP

require the approval of the Representatives of all Consultative Parties present at the Meeting.

Annex

Procedures for the Submission, Translation and Distribution of Documents for the ATCM and the CEP

1.   These procedures apply to the submission, translation and distribution of official papers for the Antarctic Treaty Consultative Meeting (ATCM) and for the Committee on Environmental Protection (CEP) as defined in their respective Rules of Procedure. These papers consist of Working Papers, Secretariat Papers, Information Papers and Background Papers.

2.   Papers that are submitted to both the ATCM and the CEP should indicate, where feasible, what portions or elements of the paper should, in the opinion of the submitter, be discussed in each forum.

3.   Documents to be translated are Working Papers, Secretariat Papers, reports submitted to the ATCM by ATCM Observers and invited Experts according to the provisions of Recommendation XIII-2, reports submitted to the ATCM in relation to Article III-2 of the Antarctic Treaty, and Information Papers that a Consultative Party requests be translated. Background Papers will not be translated.

4.   Papers that are to be translated, with the exception of the reports of Intersessional Contact Groups (ICG) convened by the ATCM or CEP, Chair Reports from Antarctic Treaty Meetings of Experts, and the Secretariat's Report and Programme, should not exceed 1500 words. When calculating the length of a paper, proposed Measures, Decisions and Resolutions and their attachments are not included.

5.   Papers that are to be translated should be received by the Secretariat no later than 45 days before the Consultative Meeting. If any such paper is submitted later than 45 days before the Consultative Meeting, it may only be considered if no Consultative Party objects.

6.   The Secretariat should receive Information Papers for which no translation has been requested and Background Papers that participants wish to be listed in the Final Report no later than 30 days before the Meeting.

7.   The Secretariat will indicate on each document submitted by a Contracting Party, an Observer, or an Expert the date it was submitted.

8.   When a revised version of a Paper made after its initial submission is resubmitted to the Secretariat for translation, the revised text should indicate clearly the amendments that have been incorporated.

9.   The Papers should be transmitted to the Secretariat by electronic means and will be uploaded to the ATCM Home Page established by the Secretariat. Working Papers received before the 45 day limit should be uploaded as soon as possible and in any case not later than 30 days before the Meeting. Papers will be uploaded initially to the password protected portion of the website, and moved to the non-password protected part once the Meeting has concluded.

10.   Parties may agree to present any paper for which a translation has not been requested to the Secretariat during the Meeting for translation.

11.   No paper submitted to the ATCM should be used as the basis for discussion at the ATCM or at the CEP unless it has been translated into the four official languages.

12.   Within three months of the end of the Consultative Meeting, the Secretariat will post on the ATCM Home Page a preliminary version of the Final Report of the Meeting in the four official languages. This version of the report shall be clearly marked "PRELIMINARY" and shall indicate that it is subject to final formatting, editing, and publishing processes.

13.   Within six months of the end of the Consultative Meeting, the Secretariat will circulate to Parties and also post on the ATCM Home Page the Final Report of that Meeting in the four official languages.

Revised Rules of Procedure for the Committee for Environmental Protection (2011)

Rule 1

Where not otherwise specified the Rules of Procedure for the Antarctic Treaty Consultative Meeting shall be applicable.

Rule 2

For the purposes of these Rules of Procedure:

a) the expression "Protocol" means the Protocol on Environmental Protection to the Antarctic Treaty, signed in Madrid on 4 October, 1991;
b) the expression "the Parties" means the Parties to the Protocol;
c) the expression "Committee" means the Committee for Environmental Protection as defined in Article 11 of the Protocol;
d) the expression "Secretariat" means the Secretariat of the Antarctic Treaty.

Part I Representatives and Experts

Rule 3

Each Party to the Protocol is entitled to be a member of the Committee and to appoint a representative who may be accompanied by experts and advisers with suitable scientific, environmental or technical competence.

Before each meeting of the Committee each member of the Committee shall, as early as possible, notify the Host Government of that meeting of the name and designation of each representative, and before or at the beginning of the meeting, the name and designation of each expert and adviser.

Part II Observers and Consultation

Rule 4

Observer status in the Committee shall be open to:

a) any Contracting Party to the Antarctic Treaty which is not a Party to the Protocol;
b) the President of the Scientific Committee on Antarctic Research, the Chairman of the Scientific Committee for the Conservation of Antarctic Marine Living Resources and the Chairman of the Council of Managers of National Antarctic Programmes, or their nominated Representatives;

c) subject to the specific approval of the Antarctic Treaty Consultative Meeting, other relevant scientific, environmental and technical organisations which can contribute to the work of the Committee.

Rule 5

Before each meeting of the Committee each observer shall, as early as possible, notify the Host Government of that meeting of the name and designation of its representative attending the meeting.

Rule 6

Observers may participate in the discussions, but shall not participate in the taking of decisions.

Rule 7

In carrying out its functions the Committee shall, as appropriate, consult with the Scientific Committee on Antarctic Research, the Scientific Committee for the Conservation of Antarctic Marine Living Resources, the Council of Managers of National Antarctic Programmes and other relevant scientific, environmental and technical organisations.

Rule 8

The Committee may seek the advice of experts as required on an ad hoc basis.

Part III Meetings

Rule 9

The Committee shall meet once a year, generally and preferably in conjunction with the Antarctic Treaty Consultative Meeting and at the same location. With the agreement of the ATCM, and in order to fulfill its functions, the Committee may also meet between annual meetings.

The Committee may establish informal open-ended contact groups to examine specific issues and report back to the Committee.

Open-ended contact groups established to undertake work during intersessional periods shall operate as follows:

a) where appropriate, the contact group coordinator shall be agreed by the Committee during its meeting and noted in its final report;
b) where appropriate, the terms of reference for the contact group shall be agreed by the Committee and included in its final report;

c) where appropriate, the modes of communication for the contact group, such as e-mail, the online discussion forum maintained by the Secretariat and informal meetings, shall be agreed by the Committee and included in its final report;

d) representatives who wish to be involved in a contact group shall register their interest with the coordinator through the discussion forum, by e-mail or by other appropriate means;

e) the coordinator shall use appropriate means to inform all group members of the composition of the contact group;

f) all correspondence shall be made available to all members of the contact group in a timely manner; and

g) when providing comments, members of the contact group shall state for whom they are speaking.

The Committee may also agree to establish other informal sub-groups or to consider other ways of working such as, but not limited to, workshops and video-conferences.

Rule 10

The Committee may establish, with the approval of the Antarctic Treaty Consultative Meeting, subsidiary bodies, as appropriate.

Such subsidiary bodies shall operate on the basis of the Rules of Procedure of the Committee as applicable.

Rule 11

The Rules of Procedure for the preparation of the Agenda of the Antarctic Treaty Consultative Meeting shall apply with necessary changes to Committee meetings.

Before each meeting of any subsidiary body the Secretariat, in consultation with the Chairperson of both the Committee and of the subsidiary body, shall prepare and distribute a preliminary annotated Agenda.

Part IV Submission of Documents

Rule 12

1. Working Papers shall refer to papers submitted by Members of the Committee that require discussion and action at a Meeting and papers submitted by Observers referred to in Rule 4(b).

2. Secretariat Papers shall refer to papers prepared by the Secretariat pursuant to a mandate established at a Meeting, or which would, in the view of the Executive Secretary, help inform the Meeting or assist in its operation.

3. Information Papers shall refer to:

- Papers submitted by Members of the Committee or Observers referred to in Rule 4(b) that provide information in support of a Working Paper or that are relevant to discussions at a Meeting;
- Papers submitted by Observers referred to in Rule 4(a) that are relevant to discussions at a Meeting; and
- Papers submitted by Observers referred to in Rule 4(c) that are relevant to discussions at a Meeting.

4. Background Papers shall refer to papers submitted by any participant that will not be introduced in a Meeting, but that are submitted for the purpose of formally providing information.

5. Procedures for the submission, translation and distribution of documents are annexed to the ATCM Rules of Procedure.

Part V Advice and Recommendations

Rule 13

The Committee shall try to reach consensus on the recommendations and advice to be provided by it pursuant to the Protocol.

Where consensus cannot be achieved the Committee shall set out in its report all views advanced on the matter in question.

Part VI Decisions

Rule 14

Where decisions are necessary, decisions on matters of substance shall be taken by a consensus of the members of the Committee participating in the meeting. Decisions on matters of procedure shall be taken by a simple majority of the members of the Committee present and voting. Each member of the Committee shall have one vote. Any question as to whether an issue is a procedural one shall be decided by consensus.

Part VII Chairperson and Vice-chairs

Rule 15

The Committee shall elect a Chairperson and two Vice-chairs from among the Consultative Parties. The Chairperson and the Vice-chairs shall be elected for a period of two years and, where possible, their terms shall be staggered.

The Chairperson and the Vice-chairs shall not be re-elected to their post for more than one additional two-year term. The Chairperson and Vice-chairs shall not be representatives from the same Party.

The Vice-chair who has been a Vice-chair for the longer period of time (in total, counting any previous term of office) shall be first Vice-chair.

In the event that both Vice-chairs are appointed for the first time at the same meeting, the Committee shall determine which Vice-chair is elected as first Vice-chair.

Rule 16

Amongst other duties the Chairperson shall have the following powers and responsibilities:

a) convene, open, preside at and close each meeting of the Committee;
b) make rulings on points of order raised at each meeting of the Committee provided that each representative retains the right to request that any such decision be submitted to the Committee for approval;
c) approve a provisional agenda for the meeting after consultation with Representatives;
d) sign, on behalf of the Committee, the report of each meeting;
e) present the report referred to in Rule 22 on each meeting of the Committee to the Antarctic Treaty Consultative Meeting;
f) as required, initiate intersessional work; and
g) as agreed by the Committee, represent the Committee in other forums.

Rule 17

Whenever the Chairperson is unable to act, the first Vice-chair shall assume the powers and responsibilities of the Chairperson.

Whenever both the Chair and first Vice-chair are unable to act, the second Vice-chair shall assume the powers and responsibilities of the Chairperson.

Rule 18

In the event of the office of the Chairperson falling vacant between meetings, the first Vice-chair shall exercise the powers and responsibilities of the Chairperson until a new Chairperson is elected.

If the offices of both the Chairperson and first Vice-chair fall vacant between meetings, the second Vice-chair shall exercise the powers and responsibilities of the Chairperson until a new Chairperson is elected.

Rule 19

The Chairperson and Vice-chairs shall begin to carry out their functions on the conclusion of the meeting of the Committee at which they have been elected.

Part VIII Administrative Facilities

Rule 20

As a general rule the Committee, and any subsidiary bodies, shall make use of the administrative facilities of the Government which agrees to host its meetings.

Part IX Languages

Rule 21

English, French, Russian and Spanish shall be the official languages of the Committee and, as applicable, the subsidiary bodies referred to in Rule 10.

Part X Records and Reports

Rule 22

The Committee shall present a report on each of its meetings to the Antarctic Treaty Consultative Meeting. The report shall cover all matters considered at the meeting of the Committee, including at its intersessional meetings and by its subsidiary bodies as appropriate, and shall reflect the views expressed. The report shall also include a comprehensive list of the officially circulated Working Papers, Information Papers and Background Papers. The report shall be presented to the Antarctic Treaty Consultative Meeting in the official languages. The report shall be circulated to the Parties, and to observers attending the meeting, and shall thereupon be made publicly available.

Part XI Amendments

Rule 23

The Committee may adopt amendments to these rules of procedure, which shall be subject to approval by the Antarctic Treaty Consultative Meeting

Parties

The original Signatories to the Treaty are the twelve countries that were active in Antarctica during the International Geophysical Year of 1957-58 and then accepted the invitation of the Government of the United States of America to participate in the diplomatic conference at which the Treaty was negotiated in Washington in 1959. These Parties have the right to participate in the meetings provided for in Article IX of the Treaty (Antarctic Treaty Consultative Meetings, ATCM).

Since 1959, 41 other countries have acceded to the Treaty. According to Art. IX.2, they are entitled to participate in the Consultative Meetings during such times as they demonstrate their interest in Antarctica by *"conducting substantial research activity there"*. Seventeen of the acceding countries have had their activities in Antarctica recognized according to this provision, and consequently there are now twenty-nine Consultative Parties in all. The other 24 Non-Consultative Parties are invited to attend the Consultative Meetings but do not participate in the decision-making.

The following table shows:

- The date on which the Treaty entered into force for each Party. In the case of the original Parties, this is 23 June 1961, whereas in the case of countries acceding later, it is the date on which they deposited their instrument of accession.
- The consultative status of the original Parties (marked by an asterisk *), which is permanent and dates from the entry into force of the Treaty: 23 June 1961. For the other Parties, the date listed is the date on which the consultative status of the Party was recognized by the ATCM.
- The date of the entry into force of the Environment Protocol for each Party. The Protocol first entered into force on 14 January 1998.
- Countries party to the Convention for the Conservation of Antarctic Seals (CCAS) or the Convention for the Conservation of Antarctic Marine Living Resources (CCAMLR) indicated with a check mark.

Country	Entry into force	Consultative status	Environment Protocol	CCAS	CCAMLR
Argentina*	23 Jun 1961	23 Jun 1961	14 Jan 1998	X	X
Australia*	23 Jun 1961	23 Jun 1961	14 Jan 1998	X	X
Austria	25 Aug 1987				
Belarus	27 Dec 2006		15 Aug 2008		
Belgium*	23 Jun 1961	23 Jun 1961	14 Jan 1998	X	X
Brazil	16 May 1975	27 Sep 1983	14 Jan 1998	X	X
Bulgaria	11 Sep 1978	05 Jun 1998	21 May 1998		X
Canada	04 May 1988		13 Dec 2003	X	X
Chile*	23 Jun 1961	23 Jun 1961	14 Jan 1998	X	X
China	08 Jun 1983	07 Oct 1985	14 Jan 1998		X
Colombia	31 Jan 1989				
Cuba	16 Aug 1984				
Czech Republic	14 Jun 1962	01 Apr 2014	24 Sep 2004		
Denmark	20 May 1965				
Ecuador	15 Sep 1987	19 Nov 1990	14 Jan 1998		
Estonia	17 May 2001				
Finland	15 May 1984	20 Oct 1989	14 Jan 1998		X

Country	Entry into force	Consultative status	Environment Protocol	CCAS	CCAMLR
France*	23 Jun 1961	23 Jun 1961	14 Jan 1998	X	X
Germany	05 Feb 1979	03 Mar 1981	14 Jan 1998	X	X
Greece	08 Jan 1987		14 Jan 1998		X
Guatemala	31 Jul 1991				
Hungary	27 Jan 1984				
Iceland	13 Oct 2015				
India	19 Aug 1983	12 Sep 1983	14 Jan 1998		X
Italy	18 Mar 1981	05 Oct 1987	14 Jan 1998	X	X
Japan*	23 Jun 1961	23 Jun 1961	14 Jan 1998	X	X
Kazakhstan	27 Jan 2015				
Korea (DPRK)	21 Jan 1987				
Korea (ROK)	28 Nov 1986	09 Oct 1989	14 Jan 1998		X
Malaysia	31 Oct 2011		14 Sep 2016		
Monaco	31 May 2008		31 Jul 2009		
Mongolia	23 Mar 2015				
Netherlands	30 Mar 1967	19 Nov 1990	14 Jan 1998		X
New Zealand*	23 Jun 1961	23 Jun 1961	14 Jan 1998		X

Country	Entry into force	Consultative status	Environment Protocol	CCAS	CCAMLR
Norway*	23 Jun 1961	23 Jun 1961	14 Jan 1998	X	X
Pakistan	01 Mar 2012		31 Mar 2012		X
Papua New Guinea	16 Mar 1981				
Peru	10 Apr 1981	09 Oct 1989	14 Jan 1998		X
Poland	23 Jun 1961	29 Jul 1977	14 Jan 1998	X	X
Portugal	29 Jan 2010		10 Oct 2014		
Romania	15 Sep 1971		05 Mar 2003		
Russian Federation*	23 Jun 1961	23 Jun 1961	14 Jan 1998	X	X
Slovak Republic	01 Jan 1993				
South Africa*	23 Jun 1961	23 Jun 1961	14 Jan 1998	X	X
Spain	31 Mar 1982	21 Sep 1988	14 Jan 1998		X
Sweden	24 Apr 1984	21 Sep 1988	14 Jan 1998		X
Switzerland	15 Nov 1990				
Turkey	24 Jan 1996				
Ukraine	28 Oct 1992	04 Jun 2004	24 Jun 2001		X

Country	Entry into force	Consultative status	Environment Protocol	CCAS	CCAMLR
United Kingdom*	23 Jun 1961	23 Jun 1961	14 Jan 1998	X	X
United States*	23 Jun 1961	23 Jun 1961	14 Jan 1998	X	X
Uruguay	11 Jan 1980	07 Oct 1985	14 Jan 1998		X
Venezuela	24 Mar 1999		31 Aug 2014		

Meetings

Every year the original twelve Parties to the Treaty and those Parties that demonstrate their interest in Antarctica by conducting substantial research activity there - together called the Consultative Parties - meet *"for the purpose of exchanging information, consulting together on matters of common interest pertaining to Antarctica, and formulating and considering and recommending to their Governments measures in furtherance of the principles and objectives of the Treaty"* (Art. IX). This forum is the Antarctic Treaty Consultative Meeting (ATCM).

The entry into force of the Environment Protocol in 1998 saw the establishment of the Committee for Environmental Protection (CEP). The CEP usually meets concurrently with the ATCM to address matters relating to environmental protection and management and provide advice to the ATCM. Besides the regular ATCM and CEP meetings, the Consultative Parties also convene occasional Special Antarctic Treaty Consultative Meetings (SATCM) and Meetings of Experts (ME) to address specific subjects.

Meeting	Dates	Location
ATCM XXXIX - CEP XIX	23 May 2016 - 01 Jun 2016	Santiago, Chile
ATCM XXXVIII - CEP XVIII	01 Jun 2015 - 10 Jun 2015	Sofia, Bulgaria
ATCM XXXVII - CEP XVII	28 Apr 2014 - 07 May 2014	Brasilia, Brazil
ATCM XXXVI - CEP XVI	20 May 2013 - 29 May 2013	Brussels, Belgium
ATCM XXXV - CEP XV	11 Jun 2012 - 20 Jun 2012	Hobart, Australia
ATCM XXXIV - CEP XIV	20 Jun 2011 - 01 Jul 2011	Buenos Aires, Argentina
ATCM XXXIII - CEP XIII	03 May 2010 - 14 May 2010	Punta del Este, Uruguay

Meeting	Dates	Location
ME Climate Change	06 Apr 2010 - 09 Apr 2010	Svolvær, Norway
ME Ship-borne Tourism	09 Dec 2009 - 11 Dec 2009	Wellington, New Zealand
ATCM XXXII - CEP XII	06 Apr 2009 - 17 Apr 2009	Baltimore, United States
ATCM XXXI - CEP XI	02 Jun 2008 - 13 Jun 2008	Kyiv, Ukraine
ATCM XXX - CEP X	30 Apr 2007 - 11 May 2007	New Delhi, India
ATCM XXIX - CEP IX	12 Jun 2006 - 23 Jun 2006	Edinburgh, United Kingdom
ATCM XXVIII - CEP VIII	06 Jun 2005 - 17 Jun 2005	Stockholm, Sweden
ATCM XXVII - CEP VII	24 May 2004 - 04 Jun 2004	Capetown, South Africa
ME Tourism	22 Mar 2004 - 25 Mar 2004	Tromsø, Norway
ATCM XXVI - CEP VI	09 Jun 2003 - 20 Jun 2003	Madrid, Spain
ATCM XXV - CEP V	10 Sep 2002 - 20 Sep 2002	Warsaw, Poland
ATCM XXIV - CEP IV	09 Jul 2001 - 20 Jul 2001	St. Petersburg, Russian Federation
SATCM XII - CEP III	11 Sep 2000 - 15 Sep 2000	The Hague, Netherlands

Meeting	Dates	Location
ME Shipping	17 Apr 2000 - 19 Apr 2000	London, United Kingdom
ATCM XXIII - CEP II	24 May 1999 - 04 Jun 1999	Lima, Peru
ATCM XXII - CEP I	25 May 1998 - 05 Jun 1998	Tromsø, Norway
ATCM XXI	19 May 1997 - 30 May 1997	Christchurch, New Zealand
ATCM XX	29 Apr 1996 - 10 May 1996	Utrecht, Netherlands
ATCM XIX	08 May 1995 - 19 May 1995	Seoul, Korea (ROK)
ATCM XVIII	11 Apr 1994 - 22 Apr 1994	Kyoto, Japan
ATCM XVII	11 Nov 1992 - 20 Nov 1992	Venice, Italy
ME Environmental Monitoring	01 Jun 1992 - 04 Jun 1992	Buenos Aires, Argentina
ATCM XVI	07 Oct 1991 - 18 Oct 1991	Bonn, Germany
SATCM XI-4	03 Oct 1991 - 04 Oct 1991	Madrid, Spain
SATCM XI-3	17 Jun 1991 - 22 Jun 1991	Madrid, Spain
SATCM XI-2	22 Apr 1991 - 30 Apr 1991	Madrid, Spain

Meeting	Dates	Location
SATCM XI-1	19 Nov 1990 - 06 Dec 1990	Viña del Mar, Chile
SATCM X	19 Nov 1990 - 19 Nov 1990	Viña del Mar, Chile
ATCM XV	09 Oct 1989 - 20 Oct 1989	Paris, France
SATCM IX	09 Oct 1989 - 09 Oct 1989	Paris, France
ME Air Safety	02 May 1989 - 05 May 1989	Paris, France
SATCM VIII	20 Sep 1988 - 21 Sep 1988	Paris, France
Meeting to Review CCAS	12 Sep 1988 - 16 Sep 1988	London, United Kingdom
SATCM IV-12 Mineral Resources	02 May 1988 - 02 Jun 1988	Wellington, New Zealand
SATCM IV-11	18 Jan 1988 - 29 Jan 1988	Wellington, New Zealand
ATCM XIV	05 Oct 1987 - 16 Oct 1987	Rio de Janeiro, Brazil
SATCM VII	05 Oct 1987 - 05 Oct 1987	Rio de Janeiro, Brazil
SATCM IV-10	11 May 1987 - 20 May 1987	Montevideo, Uruguay
SATCM IV-9	27 Oct 1986 - 12 Nov 1986	Tokyo, Japan

Meeting	Dates	Location
SATCM IV-8	14 Apr 1986 - 25 Apr 1986	Hobart, Australia
ATCM XIII	08 Oct 1985 - 18 Oct 1985	Brussels, Belgium
SATCM VI	07 Oct 1985 - 07 Oct 1985	Brussels, Belgium
SATCM IV-7	23 Sep 1985 - 04 Oct 1985	Paris, France
SATCM IV-6	26 Feb 1985 - 08 Mar 1985	Rio de Janeiro, Brazil
SATCM IV-5	23 May 1984 - 31 May 1984	Tokyo, Japan
SATCM IV-4	18 Jan 1984 - 27 Jan 1984	Washington, United States
ATCM XII	13 Sep 1983 - 27 Sep 1983	Canberra, Australia
SATCM V	12 Sep 1983 - 12 Sep 1983	Canberra, Australia
SATCM IV-3	11 Jul 1983 - 22 Jul 1983	Bonn, Germany
SATCM IV-2	17 Jan 1983 - 28 Jan 1983	Wellington, New Zealand
SATCM IV-1	14 Jun 1982 - 25 Jun 1982	Wellington, New Zealand
ATCM XI	23 Jun 1981 - 07 Jul 1981	Buenos Aires, Argentina

Meeting	Dates	Location
SATCM III	03 Mar 1981 - 03 Mar 1981	Buenos Aires, Argentina
Conference on CCAMLR	07 May 1980 - 20 May 1980	Canberra, Australia
SATCM II-3	05 May 1980 - 06 May 1980	Canberra, Australia
ATCM X	17 Sep 1979 - 05 Oct 1979	Washington, United States
ME Telecommunications 3	11 Sep 1978 - 15 Sep 1978	Washington, United States
SATCM II-2	17 Jul 1978 - 28 Jul 1978	Buenos Aires, Argentina
SATCM II-1	27 Feb 1978 - 10 Mar 1978	Canberra, Australia
ATCM IX	19 Sep 1977 - 07 Oct 1977	London, United Kingdom
SATCM I	25 Jul 1977 - 29 Jul 1977	London, United Kingdom
ATCM VIII	09 Jun 1975 - 20 Jun 1975	Oslo, Norway
ATCM VII	30 Oct 1972 - 10 Nov 1972	Wellington, New Zealand
Conference on CCAS	03 Feb 1972 - 11 Feb 1972	London, United Kingdom
ATCM VI	19 Oct 1970 - 31 Oct 1970	Tokyo, Japan

Meeting	Dates	Location
ME Telecommunications 2	01 Sep 1969 - 12 Sep 1969	Buenos Aires, Argentina
ATCM V	18 Nov 1968 - 29 Nov 1968	Paris, France
ME Logistics	03 Jun 1968 - 08 Jun 1968	Tokyo, Japan
ATCM IV	03 Nov 1966 - 18 Nov 1966	Santiago, Chile
ATCM III	02 Jun 1964 - 13 Jun 1964	Brussels, Belgium
ME Telecommunications 1	24 Jun 1963 - 28 Jun 1963	Washington, United States
ATCM II	18 Jul 1962 - 28 Jul 1962	Buenos Aires, Argentina
ATCM I	10 Jul 1961 - 24 Jul 1961	Canberra, Australia
Conference on Antarctica	15 Oct 1959 - 01 Dec 1959	Washington, United States

www.ingramcontent.com/pod-product-compliance
Lightning Source LLC
Chambersburg PA
CBHW051404200326
41520CB00024B/7500